Blissful Beauty

ANTI-STRESS COLORING BOOK

Sara Muzio

Sara Muzio has more than ten years' experience working in graphic design and illustration. In 2002, after earning a degree in Medical Illustration, she began working for small graphic design studios. In 2004, she became the scientific illustrator for Lumen Edizioni, while completing a professional course in publishing and advertising graphics. From 2005 to 2011, Sara worked as a freelance graphic designer for private clients as well as public entities and publishing houses. From 2011 to 2013, she was the graphic and packaging designer for Sambonet Paderno Industrie S.p.A. Sara currently works as an illustrator and freelance graphic designer.

WHITE STAR PUBLISHERS

WS White Star Publishers® is a registered trademark
Property of White Star s.r.l.

Copyright

Copyright © 2016, 2021 White Star s.r.l.
Piazzale Luigi Cadorna, 6
20123 Milan, Italy
www.whitestar.it

Bibliographical Note

This Dover edition, first published in 2021, is a republication of the work
originally published by White Star Publishers, Milan, Italy, in 2016.

International Standard Book Number

ISBN-13: 978-0-486-84805-1
ISBN-10: 0-486-84805-1

Manufactured in China by White Star Publishers
84805101
www.doverpublications.com

2 4 6 8 10 9 7 5 3 1

2021

Blissful Beauty

ANTI-STRESS COLORING BOOK

SARA MUZIO

DOVER PUBLICATIONS, INC.
Garden City, New York

Introduction

Let your imagination take flight as you relax and color these dazzling illustrations highlighting the beauty of transformations in nature. The fanciful drawings feature a magnificent mix of plants, animals, and human figures in wonderfully detailed, dramatic designs that often surprise by revealing something unexpectedly beautiful! Sara Muzio's unique and elegant artistry will inspire your creativity and help you to replace stress with calm.

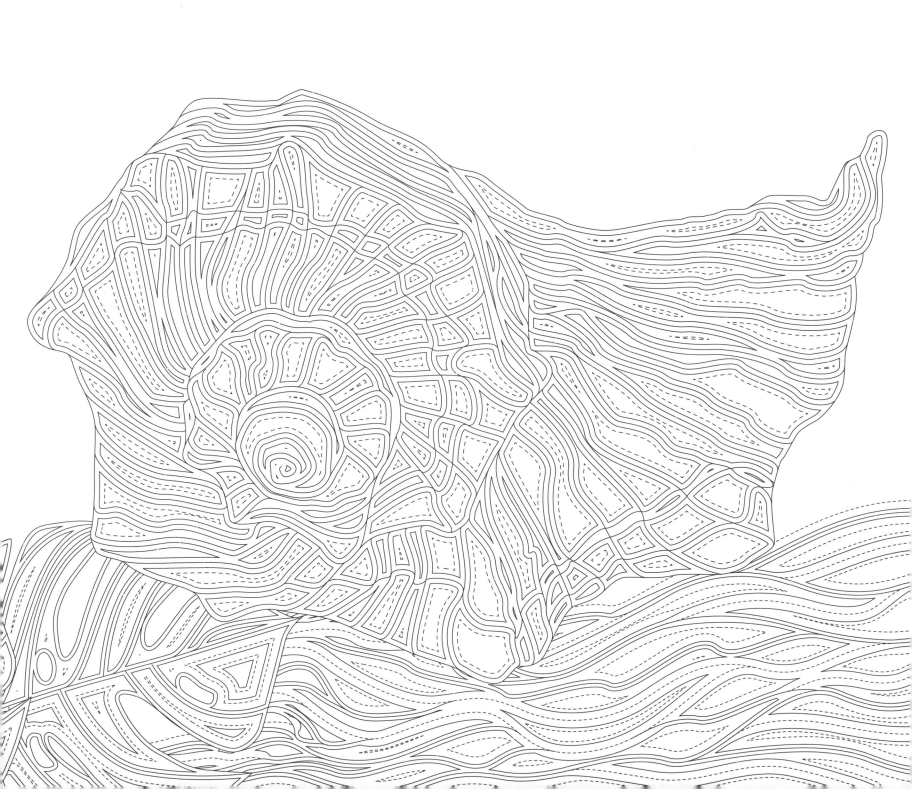

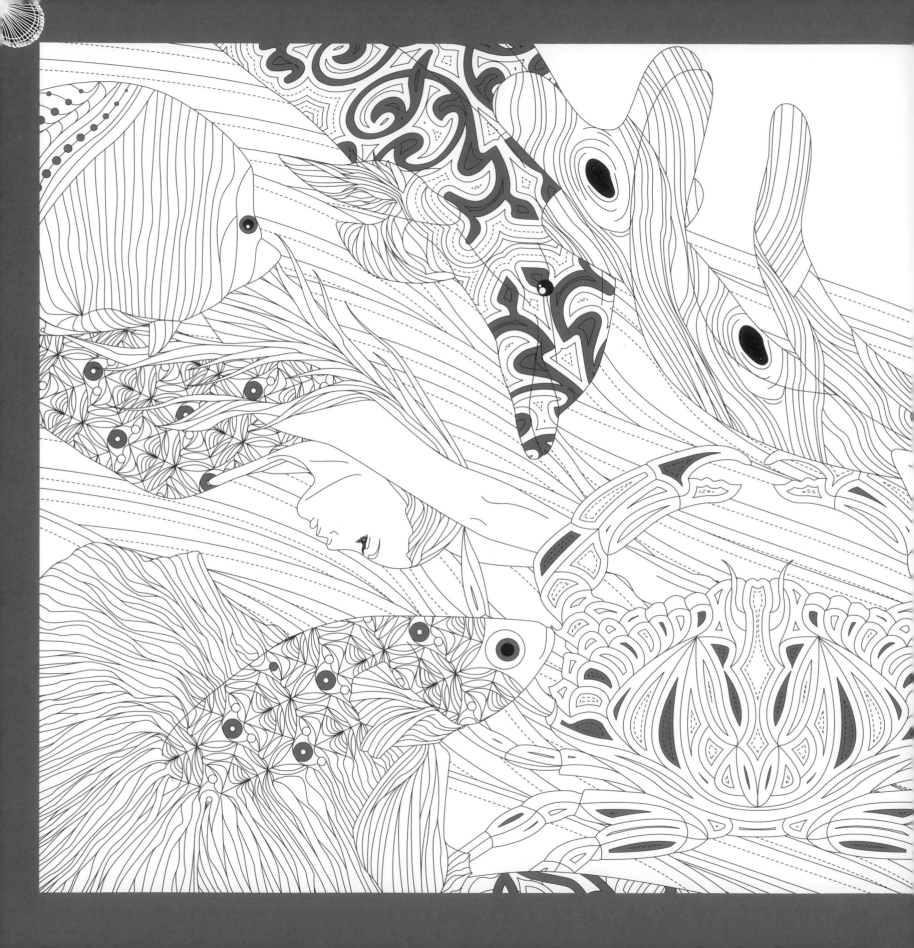

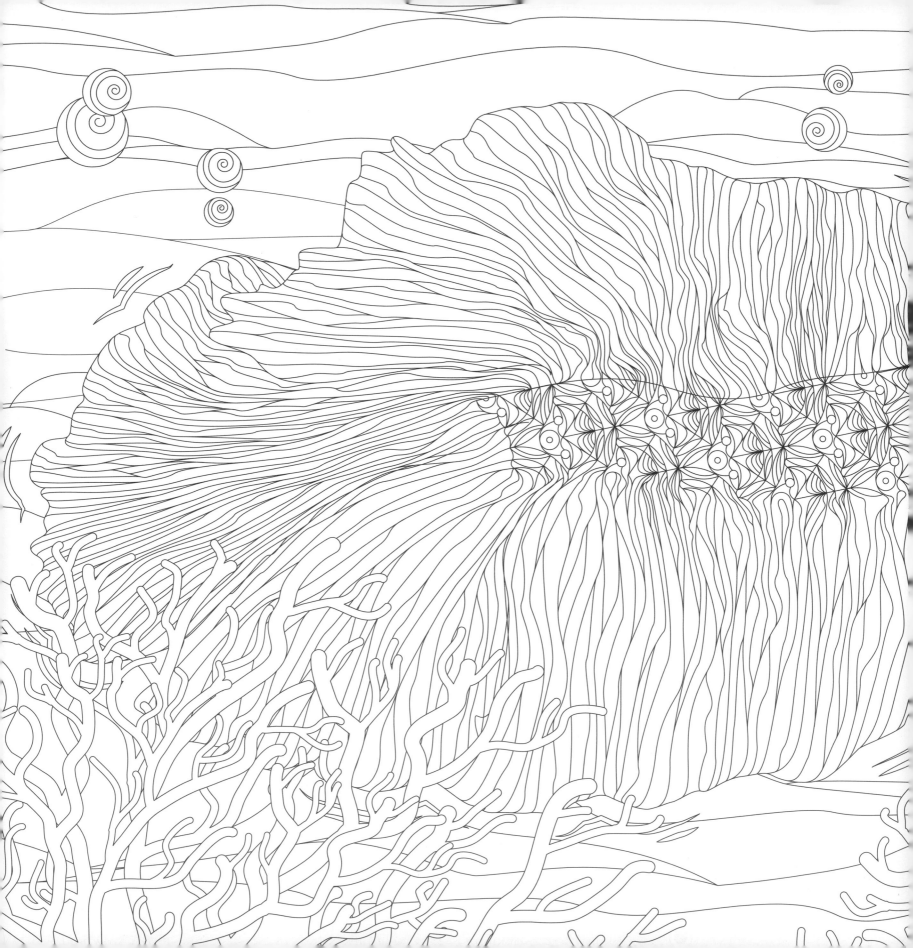

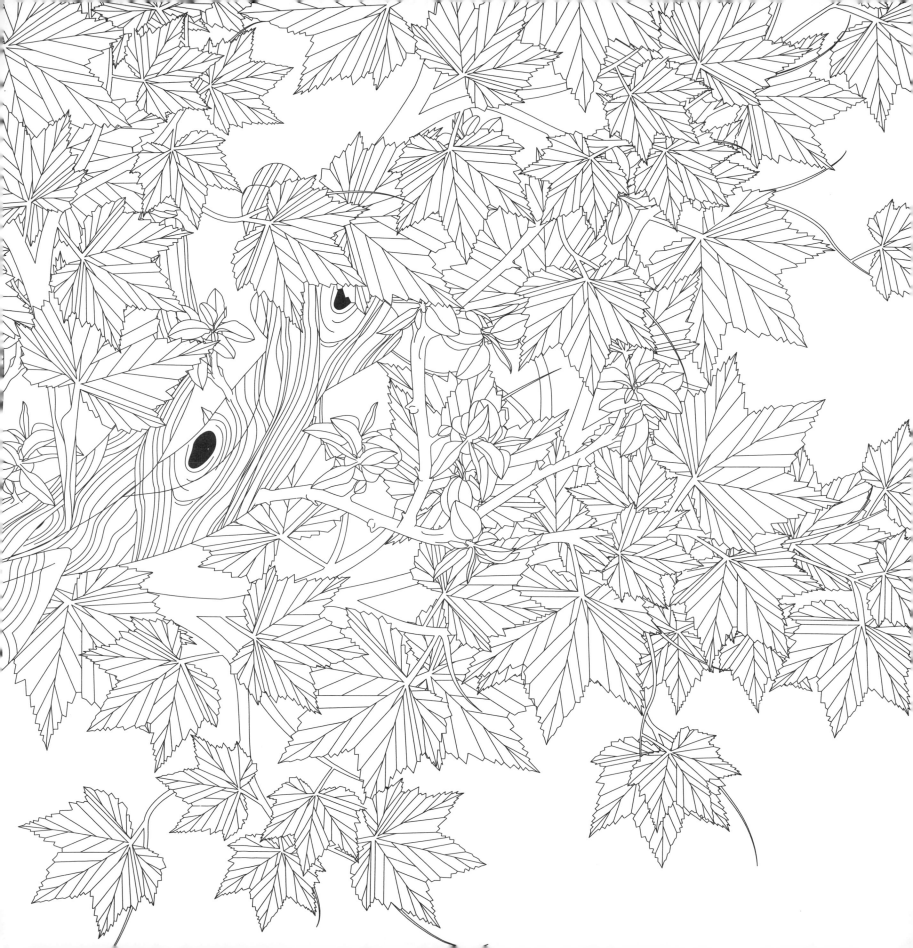

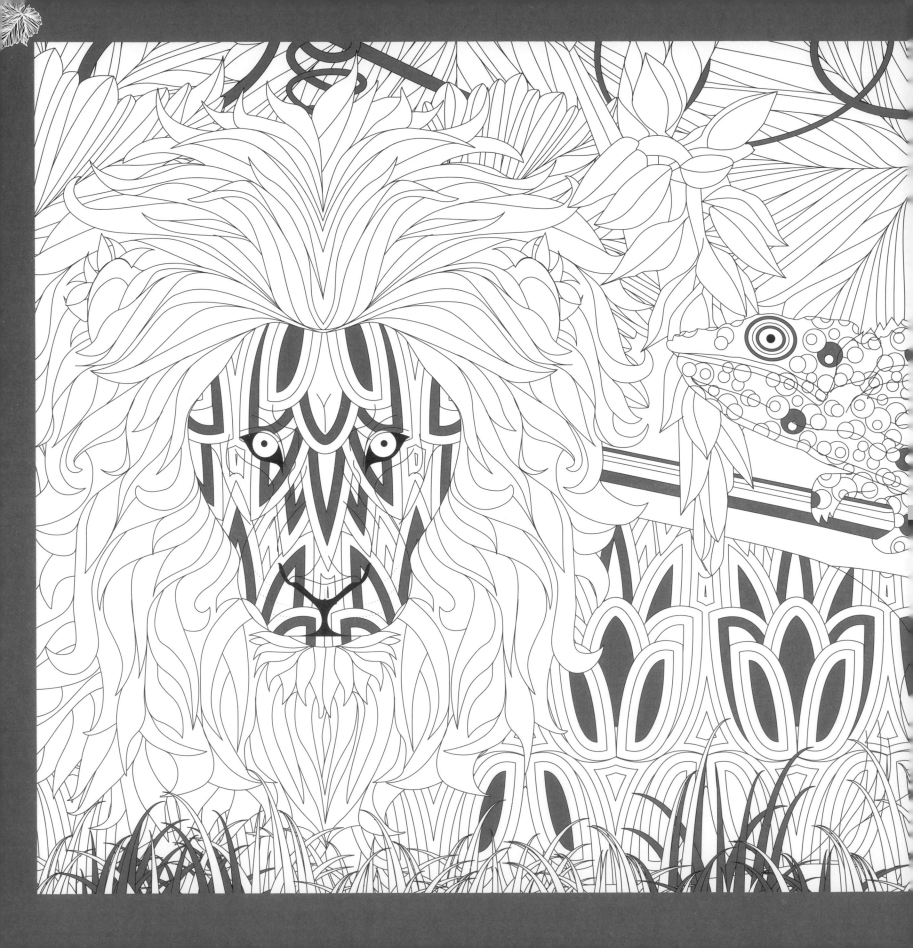